FTBC 59372097291812

WITHDRAWN

Y0-DNQ-699

WORN, SOILED, OBSOLETE

MATTHEW STAFFORD

BY JAGGER YOUSSEF

Gareth Stevens
PUBLISHING

Please visit our website, www.garethstevens.com. For a free color catalog of all our high-quality books, call toll free 1-800-542-2595 or fax 1-877-542-2596.

Library of Congress Cataloging-in-Publication Data

Names: Youssef, Jagger, author.
Title: Matthew Stafford / Jagger Youssef.
Description: New York : Gareth Stevens Publishing, [2024] | Series: Sports
  MVPs | Includes index.
Identifiers: LCCN 2023013164 (print) | LCCN 2023013165 (ebook) | ISBN
  9781538285930 (library binding) | ISBN 9781538285923 (paperback) | ISBN
  9781538285947 (ebook)
Subjects: LCSH: Stafford, Matthew, 1988–Juvenile literature. | Football
  players–United States–Biography–Juvenile literature. | Georgia
  Bulldogs (Football team)–History–Juvenile literature. | Detroit Lions
  (Football team)–History–Juvenile literature.
Classification: LCC GV939.S685 Y6 2024 (print) | LCC GV939.S685 (ebook) |
  DDC 796.33092 [B]–dc23/eng/20230413
LC record available at https://lccn.loc.gov/2023013164
LC ebook record available at https://lccn.loc.gov/2023013165

Published in 2024 by
Gareth Stevens Publishing
2544 Clinton St,
Buffalo, NY 14224

Copyright © 2024 Gareth Stevens Publishing

Designer: Claire Wrazin
Editor: Therese Shea

Photo credits: Cover, pp. 1, 17, 19 UPI/Alamy Stock Photo; pp. 5, 15 All-Pro Reels/flickr; pp. 7, 11 April Visuals/Shutterstock.com; p. 9 Associated Press/APNewsroom; pp. 13, 21 Kathy Hutchins/Shutterstock.com.

All rights reserved. No part of this book may be reproduced in any form without permission in writing from the publisher, except by a reviewer.

Printed in the United States of America

CPSIA compliance information: Batch #CS24GS: For further information contact Gareth Stevens, New York, New York at 1-800-542-2595.

Find us on

CONTENTS

Boldface words appear in the glossary.

Super Quarterback

Matthew Stafford is a quarterback in the NFL (National Football League). He holds records for the Detroit Lions, the Los Angeles Rams, and the whole NFL. In 2022, he won the biggest prize in pro football—a Super Bowl ring!

State Champ

John Matthew Stafford was born February 7, 1988, in Tampa, Florida. His family moved to Dallas, Texas. He went to Highland Park High School. He was the quarterback on the football team. In 2005, the team went **undefeated**. They won the state **championship**.

Georgia Bulldog

Matthew **graduated** high school early. He chose to go to the University of Georgia (UGA). He became the starting quarterback for the Georgia Bulldogs his first year. During his third year, he passed for 25 touchdowns, a school record.

Into the NFL

Matthew decided to leave UGA a year early. He entered the 2009 NFL **draft**. He was picked first overall by the Detroit Lions. In his first year, he became the youngest NFL quarterback to throw five touchdowns in one game.

Matthew struggled with an **injury** in 2010. But the next year, he threw for 41 touchdowns in all. The Lions made it to the playoffs too. Matthew reached 20,000 **passing yards** in just 71 games in 2014. He was chosen for the **Pro Bowl**.

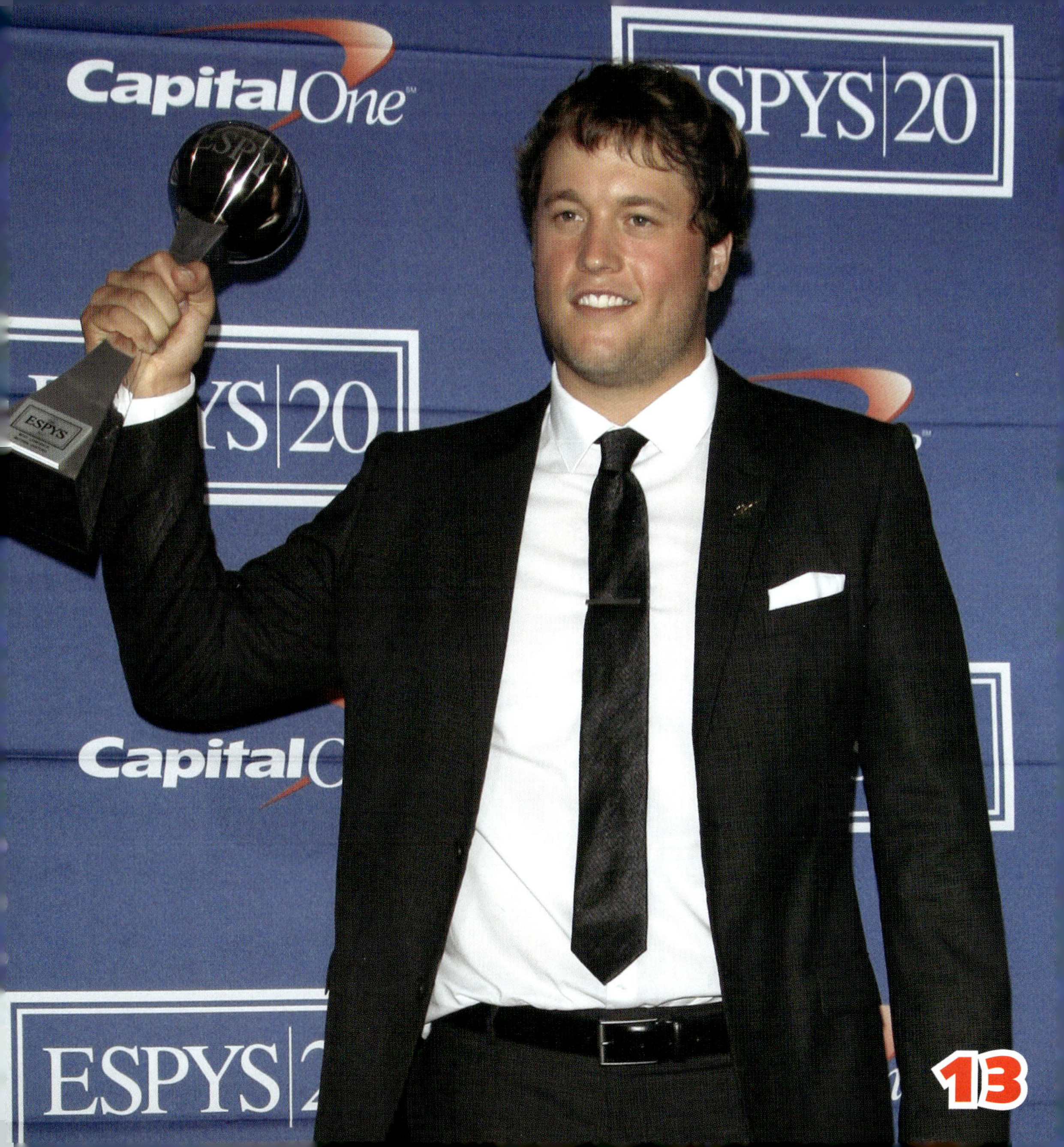
Capital One
ESPYS 20
ESPYS
ESPYS 20
Capital
ESPYS 2

Traded to LA

In 2015, Matthew was the first quarterback to complete 60 percent of his passes in all 16 games. He reached 40,000 **career** passing yards in 2019. Still, the Lions struggled to win year after year. In 2021, Matthew was traded to the Los Angeles Rams.

Super Bowl Season

During his first season, Matthew led the Rams to win the NFC (National Football Conference) West. He threw for 4,886 yards and 41 touchdowns. In the NFC Championship game, the Rams came back to win after trailing in the fourth quarter.

17

In February 2022, the Rams made it to Super Bowl LVI (56). They played the Cincinnati Bengals. The Rams were losing in the fourth quarter. But a touchdown pass from Matthew to wide receiver Cooper Kupp helped the team win, 23–20. The Rams were the NFL champions!

19

Giving Back

Off the field, Matthew and his family support many causes. He helped build a children's center in Detroit. He also gave money to UGA for **scholarships** for students in need. Matthew tries to be a leader on and off the field.

MORE TO KNOW

Matthew and his wife, Kelly, have four daughters.

He is 6 feet 3 inches (191 cm) tall.

Matthew's jersey number is 9.

He throws with his right arm.

He has an older sister named Page.

In 2022, Matthew reached 50,000 career passing yards.

GLOSSARY

career: The period of time spent in a job.

championship: A contest to decide an overall winner.

draft: The act of picking players for a team.

graduate: To earn a degree at a school.

injury: Harm or damage to the body.

passing yard: The measurement used to record how far a football is passed.

Pro Bowl: A game featuring the NFL's star players.

scholarship: Money awarded to a student to pay for their college education.

undefeated: Unbeaten.

FOR MORE INFORMATION

BOOKS

Gitlin, Marty. *The Greatest Quarterbacks of All Time.* San Diego, CA: ReferencePoint Press, 2021.

Scheff, Matt. *Matthew Stafford.* Lake Elmo, MN: Focus Readers, 2023.

Whiting, Jim. *The Story of the Detroit Lions.* Mankato, MN: Creative Education/Creative Paperbacks, 2020.

WEBSITES

Matthew Stafford
www.nfl.com/players/matthew-stafford/stats/career
Find up-to-date stats on this future hall of famer.

Matthew Stafford
www.pro-football-reference.com/players/S/StafMa00.htm
Read the latest news about this quarterback.

Publisher's note to educators and parents: Our editors have carefully reviewed these websites to ensure that they are suitable for students. Many websites change frequently, however, and we cannot guarantee that a site's future contents will continue to meet our high standards of quality and educational value. Be advised that students should be closely supervised whenever they access the internet.

INDEX